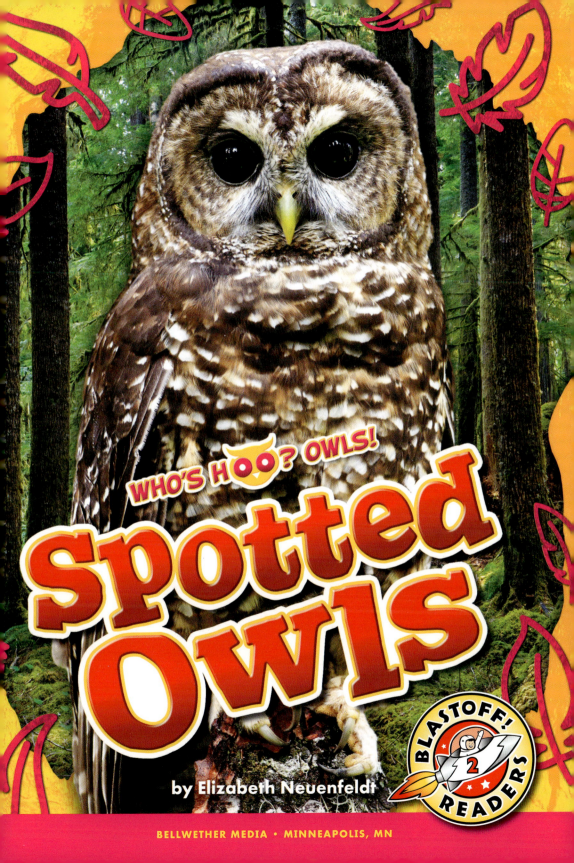

Blastoff! Readers are carefully developed by literacy experts to build reading stamina and move students toward fluency by combining standards-based content with developmentally appropriate text.

 Level 1 provides the most support through repetition of high-frequency words, light text, predictable sentence patterns, and strong visual support.

 Level 2 offers early readers a bit more challenge through varied sentences, increased text load, and text-supportive special features.

 Level 3 advances early-fluent readers toward fluency through increased text load, less reliance on photos, advancing concepts, longer sentences, and more complex special features.

★ **Blastoff! Universe**

Reading Level

This edition first published in 2024 by Bellwether Media, Inc.

No part of this publication may be reproduced in whole or in part without written permission of the publisher. For information regarding permission, write to Bellwether Media, Inc., Attention: Permissions Department, 6012 Blue Circle Drive, Minnetonka, MN 55343.

Library of Congress Cataloging-in-Publication Data

Names: Neuenfeldt, Elizabeth, author.
Title: Spotted owls / by Elizabeth Neuenfeldt.
Description: Minneapolis, MN : Bellwether Media, Inc., 2024. | Series: Blastoff! Readers. Who's Hoo? Owls! | Includes bibliographical references and index. | Audience: Ages 5-8 | Audience: Grades 2-3 | Summary: "Relevant images match informative text in this introduction to spotted owls. Intended for students in kindergarten through third grade"-- Provided by publisher.
Identifiers: LCCN 2023008901 (print) | LCCN 2023008902 (ebook) | ISBN 9798886874174 (library binding) | ISBN 9798886876055 (ebook)
Subjects: LCSH: Spotted owl--Juvenile literature.
Classification: LCC QL696.S83 N485 2024 (print) | LCC QL696.S83 (ebook) | DDC 598.9/7--dc23/eng/20230324
LC record available at https://lccn.loc.gov/2023008901
LC ebook record available at https://lccn.loc.gov/2023008902

Text copyright © 2024 by Bellwether Media, Inc. BLASTOFF! READERS and associated logos are trademarks and/or registered trademarks of Bellwether Media, Inc.

Editor: Rebecca Sabelko   Designer: Brittany McIntosh

Printed in the United States of America, North Mankato, MN.

Table of Contents

Spotted in the Trees	4
Diving in the Night	12
Growing Up!	18
Glossary	22
To Learn More	23
Index	24

Spotted in the Trees

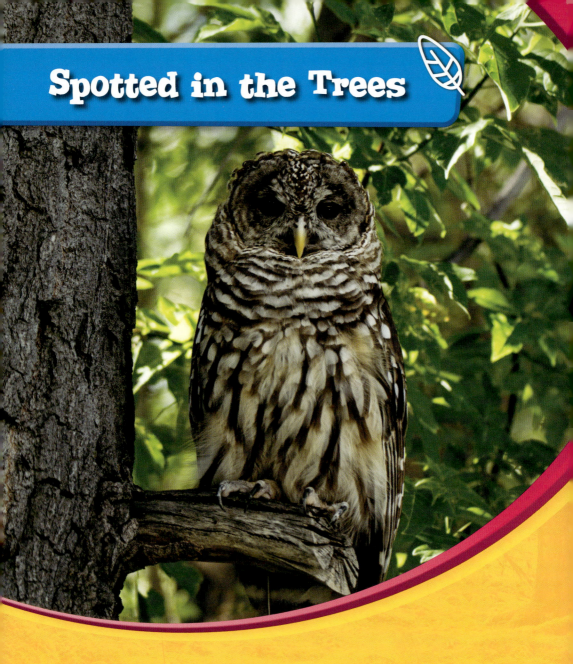

Spotted owls are named for their spotted feathers!

They are found in parts of western North America. They live in forests.

Spotted Owl Range

range = 🟩

Spotted owls have medium-sized bodies. They are around 18 inches (46 centimeters) tall.

Their **wingspan** can reach over 3 feet (1 meter) wide.

Spotted owls have dark brown feathers. White spots cover their heads, backs, and chests.

White marks make an X between their eyes.

Spotted owls have round heads.

Their eyes are large and dark. Their yellow beaks are shaped like hooks.

Spot a Spotted Owl!

- large, dark eyes
- white spots
- yellow beak

Diving in the Night

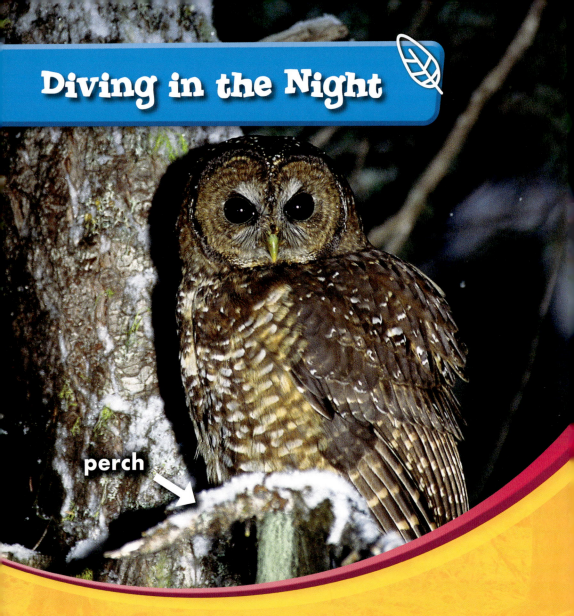

perch

Spotted owls hunt from **perches** at night. Their great hearing and eyesight help them find **prey**.

They dive silently from their perches when they find a meal.

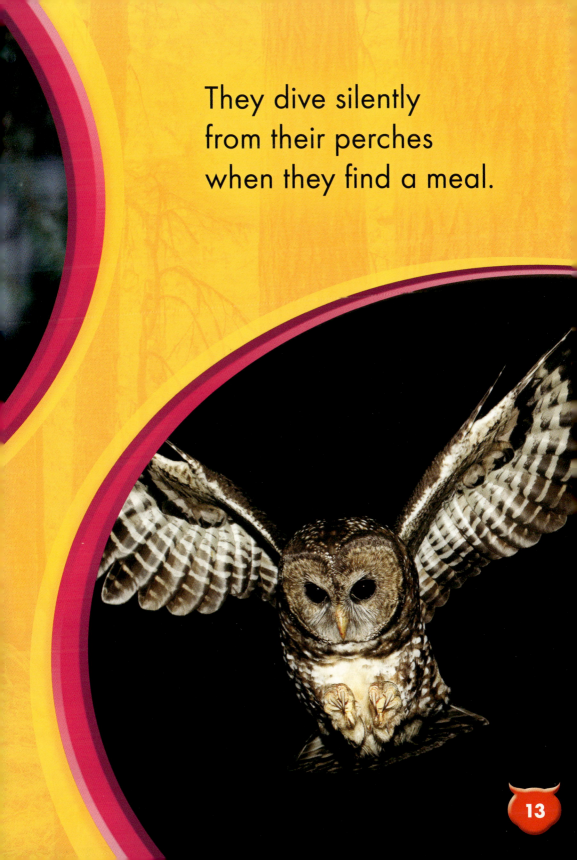

Spotted owls grab rats, squirrels, and other **rodents** with their sharp **talons**.

These owls **cache** extra food. They store meals in trees or between rocks.

rodent

Spotted Owl Food

woodrats

flying squirrels

talons

Spotted owls must watch out for **predators**. Other birds may attack or eat their eggs.

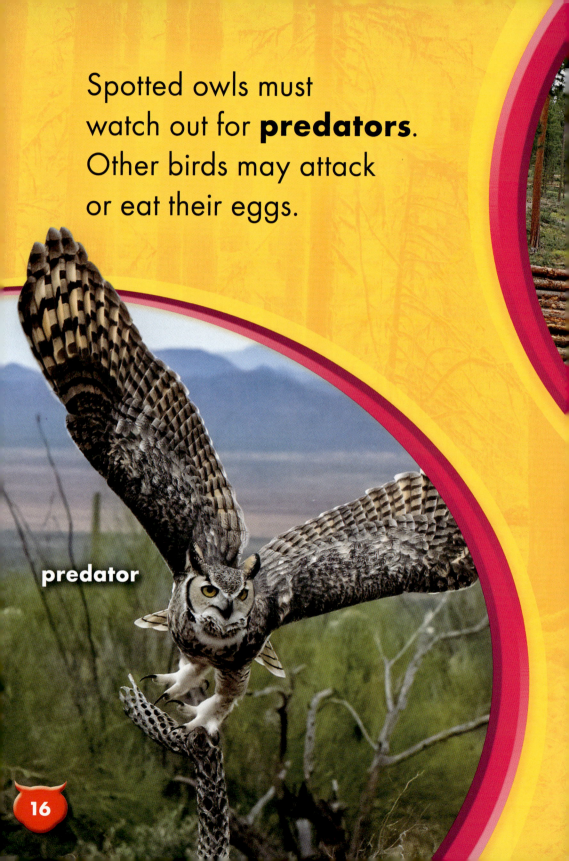

predator

People also harm the owls. They cut down forests and destroy owl **habitats**.

Growing Up!

Males and females **mate** in spring. Females usually lay one to four eggs.

Males bring females food.

Owlets come out of their eggs in about four weeks. They cannot fly yet.

Owlets become **fledglings** in about one month. Soon spotted owls live on their own!

owlet

Growing Up

1. egg — around 4 weeks
2. owlet — 4 to 5 weeks
3. fledgling — 2 to 3 months

life span: up to 21 years

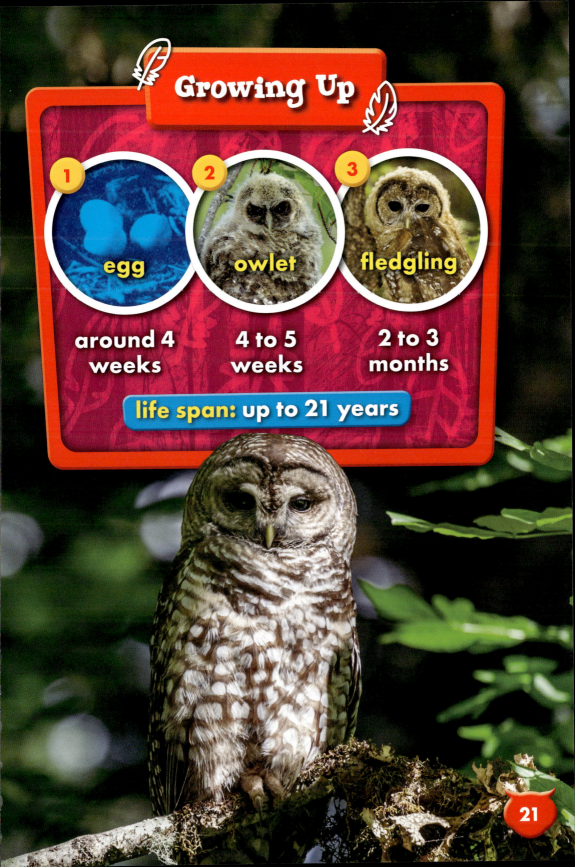

Glossary

cache—to hide or store food

fledglings—young owls that have feathers for flight

habitats—places where animals live

mate—to join together to make young

owlets—baby owls

perches—places to sit or rest above the ground

predators—animals that hunt other animals for food

prey—animals that are hunted by other animals for food

rodents—small animals that gnaw on their food; mice, rats, and squirrels are rodents.

talons—the strong, sharp claws of owls and other raptors

wingspan—the distance from the tip of one wing to the tip of the other wing

To Learn More

AT THE LIBRARY

Barnes, Rachael. *Great Horned Owls*. Minneapolis, Minn.: Bellwether Media, 2024.

Jones, Nicola. *Saving the Spotted Owl: Zalea's Story*. Toronto, Ont.: Kids Can Press, 2023.

Porter, Jane. *So You Want to Be an Owl*. Somerville, Mass.: Candlewick Press, 2021.

ON THE WEB

FACTSURFER

Factsurfer.com gives you a safe, fun way to find more information.

1. Go to www.factsurfer.com.

2. Enter "spotted owls" into the search box and click 🔍.

3. Select your book cover to see a list of related content.

Index

attack, 16
backs, 8
beaks, 11
cache, 14
chests, 8
colors, 8, 9, 11
dive, 13
eggs, 16, 18, 20
eyes, 9, 11
eyesight, 12
feathers, 4, 8
females, 18, 19
fledglings, 20
fly, 20
food, 13, 14, 15, 19
forests, 5, 17
growing up, 21
habitats, 17
heads, 8, 10
hearing, 12

hunt, 12
males, 18, 19
mate, 18
name, 4
night, 12
North America, 5
owlets, 20
perches, 12, 13
predators, 16
prey, 12
range, 5
size, 6, 7, 11
spots, 4, 8, 11
spring, 18
talons, 14, 15
wingspan, 7

The images in this book are reproduced through the courtesy of: Nature Picture Library/ Alamy, front cover, pp. 8, 11, 23; All Canada Photos/ Alamy, pp. 3, 9, 12, 13, 14, 14-15, 18, 19; Georgia Evans, p. 4; Tom Walker/ Alamy, p. 6; Wirestock, Inc./ Alamy, p. 7; twildlife, p. 10; Anton Sorokin/ Alamy, p. 15 (top left); Gerald Corsi, p. 15 (top right); Evelyn D. Harrison, p. 16; Tom Reichner, p. 17; Rick & Nora Bowers/ Alamy, p. 20; step2626, pp. 20-21; Book Worm/ Alamy, p. 21 (top left); Jared Hobbs/ All Canada Photos, p. 21 (top middle); Charles Melton/ Alamy, p. 21 (top right).